VOLCANOES

VOLCANOES

SUSAN HARRIS

An Easy-Read Fact Book

Franklin Watts
New York I London I 1979

Thanks are due to the following for kind permission to reproduce photographs:

American Museum of Natural History; Barnaby's Picture Library; John Guest; Italian State Tourist Office; Japan Airlines; New Zealand High Commission; Radio Times Hulton Picture Library; Science Museum; Scottish Tourist Board; Solarfilma; Spanish National Tourist Office; Syndication International; United States Geological Survey; United States Travel Service

Library of Congress Cataloging in Publication Data

Harris, Susan.
  Volcanoes.

  (An Easy-read fact book)
  Includes index.
  SUMMARY: Explains in simple terms different types of volcanic eruptions, the formation of vol-canoes, and the theory of plate tectonics.
    1. Volcanoes—Juvenile literature.
  [1. Volcanoes]   I. Title.
  QE522.H24   551.2′1   78-11111
  ISBN 0-531-02277-3

R.L. 2.7 Spache Revised Formula

In ancient times, people believed in many gods. The Romans believed in a god of fire. They thought he lived high up in the mountains. They believed that when he was angry, he threw fire into the sky.

Volcanic eruption on Mount Etna

Today such mountains are called **volcanoes** (vol-KA-noes). The word comes from the god's name, Vulcan.

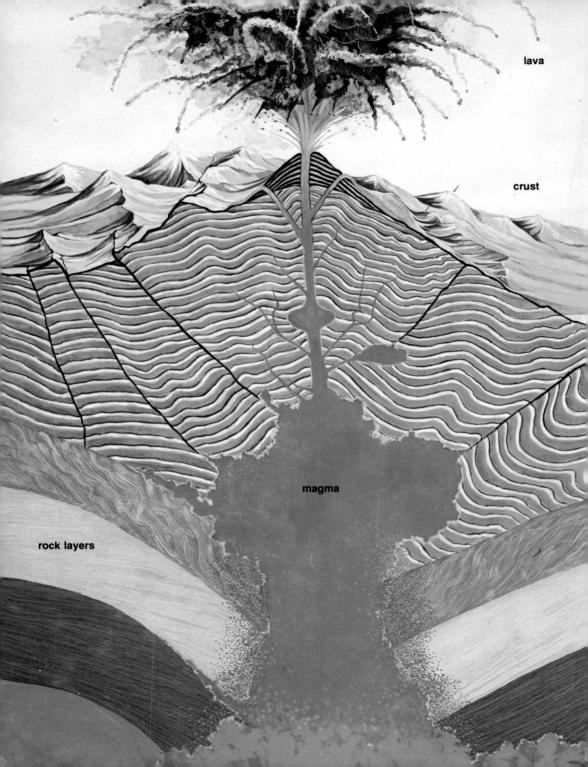

lava

crust

magma

rock layers

The earth is made up of many layers.

The top layer is called the **crust.** Under this are many layers of hard rock.

But far beneath the crust, the rock is so hot that it is soft. In some places, it actually melts.

This melted rock is called **magma**. Most of it stays safely under the crust.

But where the crust is cracked, the magma sometimes breaks through. We call this an **eruption** (e-RUP-shun). The hot magma that comes through the crust is called **lava**.

Different volcanoes erupt in different ways.

In some volcanoes, the magma is very thin and runny. When these volcanoes erupt, there is no big explosion. The lava flows gently in "rivers of fire."

The volcanoes on the island of Hawaii erupt this way.

Sometimes the lava is very runny, as in this picture of Alae Crater in Hawaii. The lava flows easily over the crater's rim.

In this picture of Surtsey, Iceland, the runny lava has divided into many branches.

A lava flow from the Mauna Ulu Crater in Hawaii. The lava has developed a thick "skin" on top. Red-hot liquid lava flows underneath.

Not all lava flows are alike. Some are thin and runny, while others are thick and pasty.

Some lava flows are mixed with dirt and stones. The lava becomes very rough, as you can see from this lava on Mount Etna. ▼

One of Hawaii's volcanoes is called Kilauea (ke-LOU-ay-a). The name means "rising smoke cloud."

Hot gas rising from a crater on Kilauea, Hawaii

During an eruption long ago, the top of the volcano fell in. This left a deep, round hole called a **crater**.

When Kilauea erupts, lava is trapped in this crater. A lake of hot lava is formed.

A crater on Hawaii filled with bubbling lava

The lava bubbles and glows in shades of red and yellow.

Sometimes a fountain of lava shoots into the air.

But not all volcanoes are as gentle as those in Hawaii.

In some volcanoes, the magma is very thick. When these volcanoes erupt, there is a big explosion.

Lava and **ash** fly high into the air.

Stromboli, an island volcano near Italy, explodes like this.

Stromboli

Tourists go to watch the explosions on Stromboli

Stromboli has been erupting for hundreds of years.
Every few minutes, a bubble of gas explodes.
Red-hot lumps of lava fly into the air.

Most of the explosions are too small to be
dangerous.

People even live in villages near the foot of
Stromboli.

Mt. Etna is a volcano on another island near Italy. It is a quiet volcano. But when it is active, it usually erupts like Stromboli.

People ski on its snowy slopes.

But in 1971, cracks opened in the mountainside. Rivers of lava poured out.

Gas became trapped inside the volcano.

Tourists visiting Mount Etna

Ashes and stones being thrown into the air
during an eruption on Mount Etna

Finally, the gas blew a hole in the rock near the top. Clouds of ash and stones blew out of this new hole.

This kind of quick "blowout" is called a **Vulcanian** (vul-KA-ne-an) **eruption**.

The city of Naples, with Mount Vesuvius in the background

A **Vesuvian** (vuh-SU-ve-an) **eruption** is as violent as a Vulcanian one. The main difference is that it lasts longer.

Its name comes from Vesuvius (vuh-SU-ve-us), a famous volcano near Naples, Italy.

This is what happens in a Vesuvian eruption: A huge cloud of gas shoots up from the top of the volcano.

The gas carries pieces of rock, lava, and ash with it.

A big eruption may cover the land with ash for miles around.

Picture of Vesuvius erupting

That is what happened in the year 79 A.D.

Vesuvius had been **dormant** (inactive) for hundreds of years.

The volcano was plugged with rock.

But there were many earthquakes between the years 62 and 79. They may have made new cracks in the rocks.

Ruins unearthed in the city of Pompeii, near Mount Vesuvius

Suddenly, in August of 79, Vesuvius erupted. Hot gases and ash made a huge black cloud over the mountain.

The eruption lasted two days.

Mosaic arch from
a villa in Pompeii

Plaster cast of a person
caught in the eruption

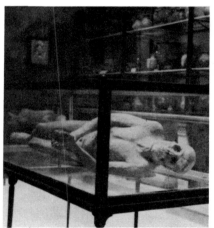

So much ash fell that the entire town of Pompeii (pom-PAY) was covered.

People were buried in 10 feet (3 m) of ash.

Most of the top of the mountain was blasted away.

Soon after the eruption, there was a rainstorm. The water turned the ash on the mountain into a thick mixture.

The wet ash flowed down the mountain. It buried the nearby town of Herculaneum (her-kyu-LAY-ne-um).

In all, two towns were buried and thousands of people died from the eruption.

Some houses unearthed in Herculaneum

Not long ago, **archaeologists** (ar-ke-OL-o-gists) (people who study ancient cultures) began to dig away at the hardened ash.

They were surprised to find two towns buried beneath.

But the towns were still in good shape. The ash had protected them from wind and rain.

So, because of the eruption, we can learn how Italians lived 1,900 years ago.

Krakatoa (kra-ka-TOE-a) is a volcanic island in Indonesia (in-doe-NE-zha). There were many earthquakes in the area early in 1883.

In May of that year, the volcano began to erupt. But the biggest bangs came in August.

They were so loud, they woke people from their sleep in southern Australia. And that's almost 2,000 miles (3,000 km) away!

Drawing of the eruption of Krakatoa

Sumatra

Krakatoa

Java

before the
eruption

Krakatoa

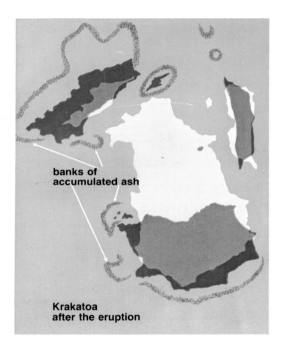

banks of
accumulated ash

Krakatoa
after the eruption

In the right-hand drawing, the pale tones show the outlines of
the islands before the eruption at Krakatoa. The present-day
shapes of the islands are in brown.

All the magma under the volcano was blown out.
This left a great hole.

The top of the volcano fell into this hole. Then the
sea poured in. The shape of the island changed.

The water around the island became so hot it
turned to steam.

Huge waves formed in the ocean.

These waves crashed onto nearby islands, killing
more than 30,000 people.

 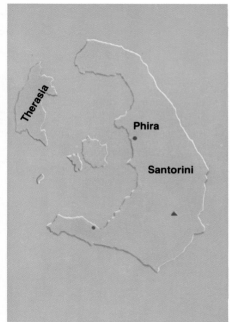

Ash from Krakatoa spread all the way around the world. So did the big waves.

But an even bigger volcano exploded 3,450 years ago. Scientists think it was about five times as powerful as the Krakatoa eruption.

It happened on an island near Greece called Santorini (san-tor-E-ne). Today, Santorini is one of a group of small islands. Long ago, they were all one island.

Santorini erupted with the biggest explosion there has ever been on earth. Part of the volcano then fell into the crater under the sea.

After the explosion at Santorini, a large part of the island collapsed into the crater. All that remains are several small islands.

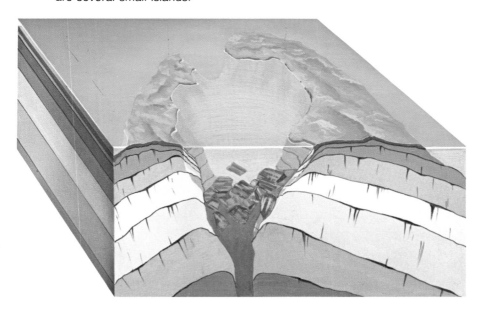

The two main islands left today are the ruin of that crater.

The eruption on Mount Pelée

There was a very unusual eruption in 1902. It happened on Mt. Pelée (pa-LAY) in the West Indies.

Very thick lava was pushed up slowly inside the volcano.

But it didn't flow out of the top. Instead, it blew a hole in the side of the mountain.

A cloud of gas shot out toward the town of St. Pierre. It moved so fast that it blew down huge walls.

The heat of the gas killed everyone in its path.

There were about 30,000 people in St. Pierre. Only two lived.

St. Pierre in ruins after Mount Pelée erupted

Even though the crust of the earth seems solid, it isn't. It is really made up of many **plates**, or pieces. The plates float like rafts on the rock below them. They all move around a little.

World map showing the position of the plates

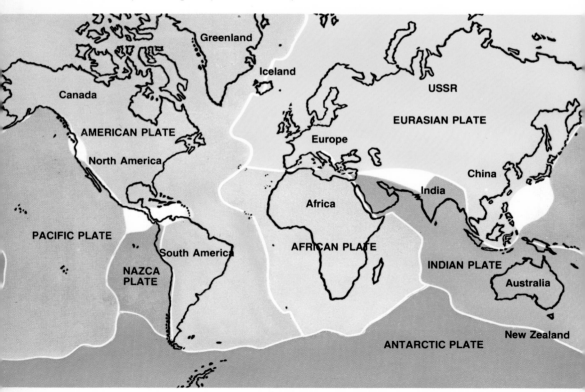

In some places, they move apart. In others, they slide past each other. In yet others, they push against each other.

There are about 500 volcanoes in the world. Almost all are in places where two plates meet.

World map showing major volcanoes

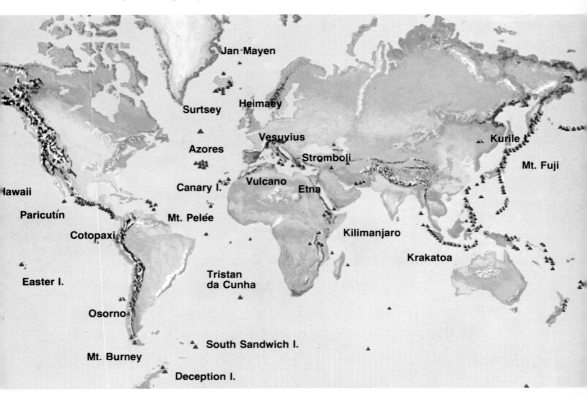

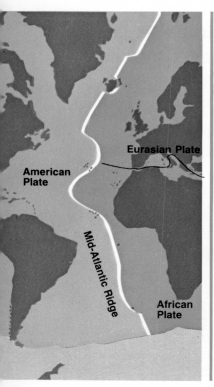

Left: the Mid-Atlantic Ridge has formed in the gap between the African and American Plates; right: volcanic scenery on one of the Canary Islands.

The African plate and the American plate are slowly moving apart. They have been moving this way for millions of years.

As they move, **molten** (hot liquid) rock from below moves between them. This has formed a **chain**, or line of volcanoes.

It runs along the line where the two plates meet.

Many of these undersea volcanoes have grown very high.

Some even stick out above the ocean to make islands.

The Azores and the Canary Islands are volcanic islands. So is Tristan da Cunha (TRIS-tan-de-COON-ya).

People escaping from Tristan da Cunha during an eruption in 1961

Hekla erupting

Iceland is another volcanic island rising out of the Atlantic Ocean.

As the plates around it move apart, Iceland grows wider. Molten rock erupts from the many volcanoes on the island.

Iceland's most famous volcano is Hekla. Its name means "black gate of hell."

Hekla last erupted about 30 years ago. Lava and ash poured out.

Ash landed in the water supply. It covered nearby meadows. The ash on the meadows began to wear away the teeth of the cows!

In 1963, a new island was born near Iceland. It was named Surtsey, after an ancient fire god.

Surtsey. Steam in the foreground
is caused by the hot lava entering the sea.

Two new islands were formed during the eruption
of Surtsey.

This picture shows Surtsey in the background.
One of the new small islands is in the foreground.
Both small islands were soon covered by the sea.

In 1973 another volcano erupted near Iceland. It was on the island of Heimaey (HAM-a-ee). All the people on the island had to leave.

Lava flowing over homes on Heimaey

They could not return for 18 months.

Five years later, in 1978, the lava was still warm. In fact, people used it to heat their homes.

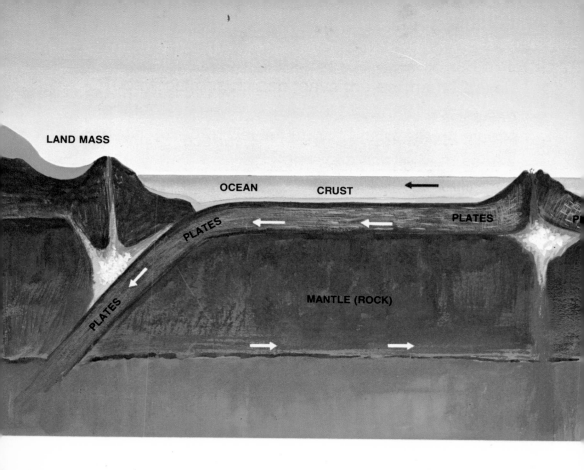

The bed of the Pacific Ocean is made of two plates. (See the maps on pages 28 and 29.)

These plates are slowly moving away from each other.

They push against the land around the edge of the Pacific Ocean.

Where the plates rub, one becomes so hot that the rocks melt.

This molten rock comes to the surface. Some of it breaks through to make volcanoes.

Around the Pacific is a chain of volcanoes. It is known as the **ring of fire**.

Japan and New Zealand are on this ring. Both of these countries have many volcanoes.

Mount Fuji, Japan

Volcanic crater of Guélletiri
in the Bolivian Andes

From Japan, the ring of fire goes up to Alaska.
Then it comes down the west coast of America.
Finally, it ends in the Andes Mountains of South
America.

There are thousands of dormant volcanoes in the
Andes. And there are almost 50 active ones as well.

Not all volcanoes look like mountains. One in
Mexico started as a small pit.

One day the pit cracked open. A small mound began to form. Soon smoke, ash, and lava poured out.

The ashes ruined crops 50 miles (80 km) away.

The young volcano was named Paricutín (PEH-re-ku-ten).

After just one week, it was 500 feet (152 m) high.

Paricutín exploding, throwing up clouds of smoke and ash

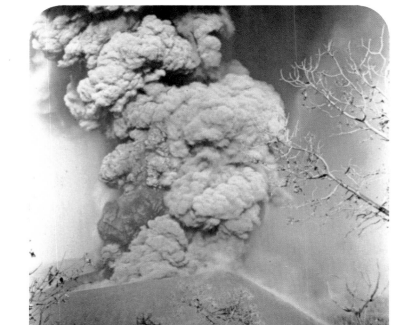

Crater Lake

Paricutín is one of the youngest volcanoes.

But there are many very old volcanoes that no longer erupt. These are said to be **extinct**.

Crater Lake in Oregon is really the crater of an old volcano.

Often there is little left to see of an old volcano.

Over the years, wind and rain wear away the volcanic rock.

But the **inner neck**, or plug, of the volcano is made of harder rock. Sometimes it lasts longer.

There are five inner necks of old volcanoes in Edinburgh, Scotland. The hill called Arthur's Seat is one of them.

Arthur's Seat

People bathing in hot springs in New Zealand

The power that makes volcanoes erupt is not always violent.

There is hot magma and gas deep underground in New Zealand. But it does not often cause eruptions.

Instead, the gas comes slowly up through the earth's crust. As it nears the surface, it heats water in the ground.

Sometimes the hot
water and steam
shoot up in a **geyser**
(GI-zer).

Sometimes they
bubble out of the
ground in a hot spring.

A geyser in
Yellowstone National Park

Sometimes they
just make pools
of bubbling mud.

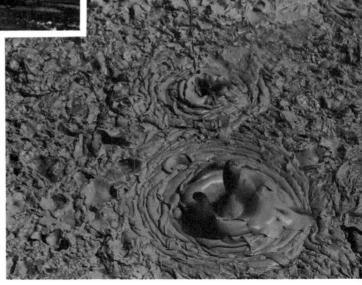

Pool of bubbling mud
in New Zealand

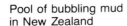

Scientists are learning to use this "gentle" energy from the earth.

They called it **geothermal** (ge-o-THER-mal) **energy**. ("Geo" means "earth," and "thermal" means "heat.")

Scientists testing the heat of lava

Geothermal–electric power station in New Zealand

Scientists hope to use geothermal energy much more in the future.

They will use the heat of molten rocks to turn water to steam.

The steam can then be used to make electricity for our homes and industries.

Producing geothermal energy by passing water
through hot rocks

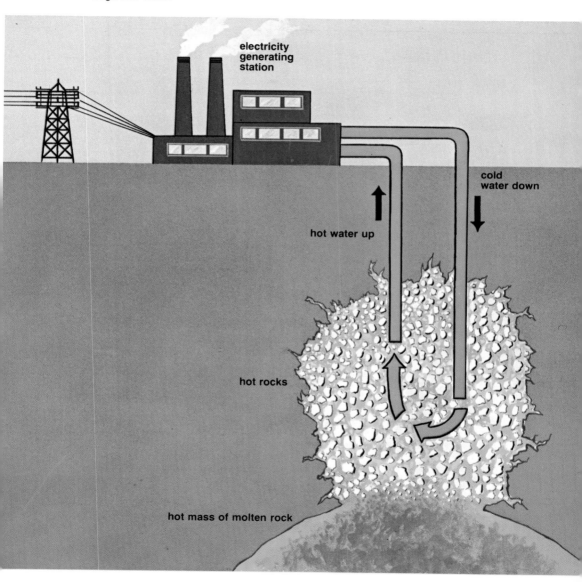

electricity
generating
station

cold
water down

hot water up

hot rocks

hot mass of molten rock

Inside a volcanic observatory

If scientists knew when a volcano was going to erupt, they could get everyone safely away.

Earthquakes often give a signal.

An instrument called a **seismometer** (size-MOM-a-ter) can "feel" even the tiniest earthquake.

Many volcanoes swell up a little before they erupt. This can be measured with a **tiltmeter**.

The drawings show how it works.

Two bowls of water far apart on the side of the volcano are joined by a pipe.

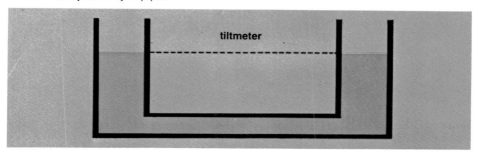

As the volcano swells, one bowl is lifted up. Some of its water runs down to the other bowl.

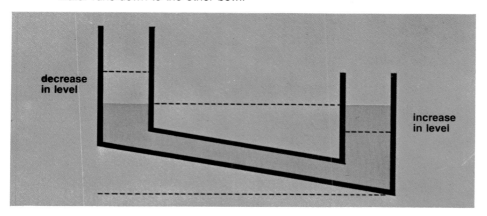

Hot magma swells up under a volcano before it erupts. This causes the rocks around it to become very hot.

By measuring this increase in heat, scientists can know when to expect a volcanic eruption.

Index